ELIZABETH TAYLOR

D1715717

T&J

Published by TAJ Books International LLC 2014
5501 Kincross Lane
Charlotte, North Carolina, USA
28277

www.tajbooks.com
www.tajminibooks.com

All notations of errors or omissions (author inquiries, permissions) concerning
the content of this book should be addressed to
info@tajbooks.com.

The Publisher wishes to thank Alan Light, LIFE magazine, John Bryson,
Toni Frissell, CityMorgue, and MGM.

ISBN 978-1-84406-263-8 Hardback
978-1-62732-002-3 Paperback

Printed in China

1 2 3 4 5 18 17 16 15 14

ELIZABETH TAYLOR

T&J

KATHRYN DIXON

We might not even know the unquestionable star that was Elizabeth Taylor if she had not been the daughter of the mother of all stage mothers. Born in Hampstead, England, a suburb of London, on February 27, 1932, Elizabeth was christened Elizabeth Rosemund Taylor by her parents, Francis Lenn Taylor and Sarah Viola Warmbrodt Taylor. Her brother, Howard, was three years her senior. Francis and Sara, who had acted before her marriage using the stage name Sara Sothern, were Americans residing in England at the time of Elizabeth's birth. Like her brother, who was also born in England, she had dual U.S./U.K. citizenship. In the mid-1960s when she was married to British citizen Richard Burton, Elizabeth renounced her citizenship—likely to keep her European earnings nontaxable in the U.S.—only to reapply after a decade when she married soon-to-be Virginia Senator John Warner in 1977.

Francis, Elizabeth's father, was an art dealer who began working in New York City for his childless uncle, Howard Young, who with his wife effectively adopted Francis. In New York City, Francis met and married Sara. He was soon transferred to another of Young's galleries in London. The family stayed in England until the outbreak of World War II when they returned to the United States, moving to Los Angeles, California, where Francis ran a new art gallery in Beverly Hills, once again bankrolled by his uncle. The proximity to Hollywood made Sara's sole quest in life—for Elizabeth to become a movie star—much easier to realize. Elizabeth's father's business, soon operating out of the posh Beverly Hills Hotel, also opened many doors of the rich and famous in the Hollywood community to the family. As in England, the Taylors enjoyed a very pleasant, well-connected lifestyle in their new southern California home.

In England, the family had lived a generous lifestyle, provided by their wealthy family friend, Victor Cazalet, who allowed them to use a cottage on his estate in the Kentish countryside. Weekends were spent at the cottage and weekdays in London. When Elizabeth was just five years old, Cazalet gave her a horse that she kept in Kent. Her equine experience (as well as her British accent) helped her win the role of Velvet Brown in her breakout movie, *National Velvet*,

in 1944. Cazalet also introduced Sara and Elizabeth to the Hollywood columnist Hedda Hopper, a friend of his, when she visited his estate in England. Once in California, Hedda was instrumental in making Elizabeth's introduction to Universal Pictures, the first studio that offered her a contract. Although the contract term was for seven years, the studio let her go after just one year.

At the same time that Elizabeth had been courted by Universal, Metro-Goldwyn-Mayer (MGM) had also been interested in her so it didn't take much for MGM to offer Elizabeth a contract once she was let go by Universal. Her first movie for MGM was *Lassie Come Home* in 1943 with co-star Roddy McDowall, who would be her life-long friend. Elizabeth's second film appearance at age 10 was in *Jane Eyre* for which she was loaned to 20th Century Fox. Her co-star Orson Welles is said to have whispered to a companion: "Remind me to be around when she grows up." Her violet eyes and double row of eyelashes gave her an eerily mature beauty even before she hit puberty.

After heavy lobbying efforts by her mother, Elizabeth won the role of Velvet Brown in *National Velvet*, co-starring with Mickey Rooney. The movie was a tremendous smash at the box office. It was followed by a string of movies—*Courage of Lassie* (another animal film), *Life with Father*, *Cynthia*, *A Date with Judy*, and *Julia Misbehaves* in 1947 and 1948—that were all quite successful. Elizabeth's last adolescent role was as Amy in *Little Women*, released in 1949.

Her first adult role was in *Conspirator* opposite Robert Taylor. Only 16, she very adequately portrayed her 21-year-old character. By this time she not only had the mien of an adult woman but the body as well. The movie failed at the box office, but Elizabeth received rave reviews. Her next film, *The Big Hangover*, released in 1950, was not a big hit either, but the next two—*Father of the Bride* and the sequel *Father's Little Dividend* in 1950 and 1951, respectively—were much more popular. In these two comedies, Elizabeth played Spencer Tracy's daughter, Kay Banks.

But the movie that made her an adult star, capable of handling the most sensual femme-fatale roles was *A Place in the Sun*, a remake of Theodore Dreiser's novel, *An American Tragedy*, only released in 1951 after a lengthy editing

A very young, lyrically beautiful Elizabeth Taylor

Early publicity for Elizabeth emphasized her affection for animals. She had her own horse in England before her family moved to California. At left, she sits astride her co-star in National Velvet, *1944. Below, Elizabeth is pictured with Lassie in the 1943 movie* Lassie Come Home.

A publicity still for Hold High the Torch, *1945*

process. George Stevens, the director and producer, twisted a lot of arms to get Elizabeth loaned out to Paramount to make the film. The outdoor scenes were shot on the banks of Lake Tahoe in 1949 when Elizabeth was just 17, still a teenager. Yet her performance of a woman so beautiful that a man would kill to have her was dead on and some critics view it as the best of her career. The film, deemed a classic, also starred Montgomery Clift and Shelley Winters. Elizabeth's next seven pictures for MGM were anything but noteworthy—except, perhaps, for her luminosity on screen.

Not until Warner Brothers' *Giant* in 1956 with co-stars James Dean and Rock Hudson did Elizabeth return to the silver screen in a role worthy of her acting range. The floodgates of substantial roles opened then and each of her next four movies, released annually from 1957 to 1960, garnered her nominations for Academy Award, Best Actress: *Raintree County*; *Cat on a Hot Tin Roof*; *Suddenly, Last Summer*; and *BUtterfield 8*. She won the Oscar for *BUtterfield 8* in which she co-starred with her then husband (husband number four) Eddie Fisher. It was the last movie

she made for MGM after being under contract with the studio for almost two decades.

Cleopatra was Elizabeth's next trip into uncharted waters. She was the first female actress to earn $1 million for a film and to take a share of the profits, in this case 10 percent. One of the most expensive films ever made, *Cleopatra* was a box office and critical success when it was released in 1963 but its producers still lost money. Not only was Rome the setting for this most elaborate of movies, but the Imperial City was also the setting for the

explosive affair between Elizabeth and Richard Burton (irreverently referred to as Liz and Dick), both married to others at the time. A second movie with Richard Burton, *The V.I.P.s,* was released the same year as *Cleopatra.*

Two years later, in 1965, the couple shared top billing in *The Sandpiper*, which was set on the coast of northern California. The next year, 1966, marked a high point in Elizabeth's career with the release of the film *Who's Afraid of Virginia Woolf?* The movie was based on the play of the same name by Edward Albee. Nominations and awards piled high for Elizabeth's performance. She won her second Best Actress Oscar as well as numerous other best actress awards from foreign film associations.

Liz and Dick made 10 films together. In addition to the previously mentioned four, they starred in *The Taming of the Shrew*, *Doctor Faustus, The Comedians*, *Boom!* and *Hammersmith Is Out*. The middle three were flops at the box office, although for the last, *Hammersmith Is Out*, Elizabeth won the Silver Bear for Best Actress at the Berlin International Film Festival. Their last movie together

was ironically *Divorce His, Divorce Hers* released in 1973, a year before the couple's first divorce.

For the following decade and a half, Elizabeth's film roles were much less remarkable, although she did win the David di Donatello Award for Best Foreign Actress (an Italian film award) for her performance in *X, Y, and Zee* in 1972 and was nominated for the Golden Globe Award for Best Actress in a Motion Picture Drama for *Ash Wednesday*, released in 1973. The movie, *The Flintstones*, released in 1994 was not Elizabeth's finest hour. She was nominated for the Razzie Award for Worst Supporting Actress.

Elizabeth finally tackled live theater with her 1981 Broadway debut in *The Little Foxes*. Two years later, she and Richard Burton shared the honors in *Private Lives*, also on Broadway. Most performances in her later years were in television. She appeared on the daytime soap *General Hospital* and played Madame Conti in the mini-series *North and South*. The television series, *Murphy Brown*, *The Nanny*, and *The Simpsons* also welcomed her for an episode each as herself.

In 1948, not yet 17 years old, Elizabeth posed for photographer Phillippe Halsman in a photo shoot for an article in LIFE magazine.

15

With her first husband, Nicky Hilton, one of the heirs of the Hilton hotel chain, on their wedding day in Los Angeles on May 6, 1950. The wedding was arranged by Metro-Goldwyn-Mayer to coincide with the release of her upcoming movie, Father of the Bride, *in which she played the bride. The marriage ended only months later. Her cream-colored, seed pearl-encrusted wedding dress, a gift from MGM, sold for $187,931 in June 2013 when auctioned by Christie's in London.*

The same photo shoot; this page, a black-and-white close-up; opposite page, a seated portrait in color

18

HER HUSBANDS

It is likely that Elizabeth would not have the notoriety she has today because of her many marriages, if it were not for the control MGM exerted over all aspects of her early life. As a teen, Elizabeth was romantically linked to Heisman Trophy winner Glenn Davis as well as the son of the U.S. Ambassador to Brazil, William Pawley. But at the early age of 18, Elizabeth was married to the first of her seven husbands, Conrad "Nicky" Hilton Jr., the heir to the Hilton hotel fortune. It is believed that the marriage was essentially a publicity stunt related to the movie *Father of the Bride*, which conveniently coincided with the marriage. The marriage also offered freedom from her domineering mother.

Elizabeth and Nicky were married in a lavish church ceremony in Los Angeles, the streets crowded with fans, on May 6, 1950. Her dress, an extravaganza of 25 yards of shell white satin decorated with bugle beads and seed pearls, took 15 people three months to make. A corset cinched Elizabeth's waist to 20 inches. The view as Elizabeth walked down the aisle must have been breathtaking as a 15-foot satin train and a 10-foot silk net veil trailed behind her.

Helen Rose, an Academy Award-winning costume designer who spent most of her career at MGM, designed the dress, which was a gift of the studio to Elizabeth. Rose also designed the wedding dress of Grace Kelly for her marriage to Prince Rainier of Monaco, as well as the wedding dress worn by Elizabeth in *Father of the Bride*. On June 26, 2013, Elizabeth's own wedding dress was sold by Christie's auction house in London for more than £120,000 ($187,931), over twice the original estimate.

Sadly, Elizabeth fled the marriage within nine months claiming that her husband was abusive and had a drinking problem. But within a year of her divorce she was married again, this time to the British actor Michael Wilding, 20 years her senior. Insiders hinted that this marriage too had been finagled by the studio, as well as by Elizabeth herself, in order to polish her tarnished public image after the disaster that was her first marriage. Her marriage to Michael, one day before her twentieth birthday on February 26, 1952, consisted of a quick trip to a registry

Those notoriously violet eyes!

Captured by LIFE magazine taking a break on the Paramount lot during the filming of A Place in the Sun, *1950*

office in London, a sharp contrast to her elegant and elaborate marriage ceremony to Nicky Hilton, although the new Mr. and Mrs. Wilding did enjoy a reception afterward at Claridge's, a luxury hotel in the heart of London's Mayfair. The bride wore a simple gray suit.

Michael and Elizabeth had first met in London while Elizabeth was making the movie *Conspirator* and renewed their friendship in 1951 during the filming of *Ivanhoe.* Both benefited from the union. Elizabeth oozed blissful domesticity that repaired her gay divorcee image, while Michael basked in the limelight of his movie star wife hoping some of the glitter would brighten his career. Without a doubt, Michael was a solicitous and caring husband, but that wasn't enough to keep Elizabeth from being tempted by other men. Eventually, she was introduced to her third husband, Mike Todd, and that spelled the end of the Wilding marriage. Elizabeth and Wilding had two sons, Michael Jr. and Christopher, during their five-year marriage.

Mike and Elizabeth had a short but tempestuous marriage during which they lived the high life, jetting from one side

of the globe to the other. They shared the success of Mike's first producing effort, the Academy Award-winning movie *Around the World in 80 Days*. The hustling, entrepreneurial Mike showered Elizabeth with furs and jewels and even a private yet named *Liz*. On March 22, 1958, on his way to New York City for a Friars' Club roast aboard the jet, he and the other three people with him died in a fiery crash in the countryside of New Mexico. If Elizabeth had not been battling a cold, she would have died alongside him. Although the two were known to be outspoken, willful, and openly argumentative, Elizabeth claimed many years later that he was one of the true loves of her life—the other being her fifth husband, Richard Burton. Elizabeth and Mike had a daughter, Liza.

A little more than a year after Mike's death, Elizabeth tied the knot with his best friend, the crooner Eddie Fisher. When they began their affair, Eddie was married to the pert actress, singer, and dancer Debbie Reynolds, a product of the MGM studio machine just like Elizabeth. The scandal that erupted as a result of their affair surprised and upset Elizabeth, but she persisted nonetheless even though

it seriously threatened her career. She was widely chastised as a self-centered home wrecker. The couple was married in a Las Vegas synagogue. The bride, having recently converted to Judaism, wore green chiffon. With time, the public's ire cooled and Elizabeth regained her crown of celebrity, even if a bit dented. Eddie's fate was sealed, however, the moment Elizabeth met the wild Welsh actor Richard Burton.

Richard Burton entered Elizabeth's life with a bang. The two carried on a shameless affair right under the nose of the Pope while in Rome to film *Cleopatra*. The Vatican blasted the couple, calling their adulterous behavior "erotic vagrancy." Richard at the time had been married to the actress Sybil Christopher for 14 years and they had two daughters. Richard, somewhat of a serial seducer, had managed to keep his conquests under wraps until he met Elizabeth Taylor and their infidelity was splashed across the world's newspapers. By all accounts, Sybil calmly accepted the situation, agreeing to divorce her husband so he was free to marry Elizabeth.

With second husband, Michael Wilding, and their first child, Michael Wilding Jr., in 1953

At the premier of The Lady with the Lamp *at the Warner Theater in London on September 22, 1951; the movie starred her soon-to-be husband, Michael Wilding.*

A film still, c. 1950

In Ivanhoe, *1952*

Elizabeth, however, was not so lucky. Eddie fought her request for a divorce hoping against hope that the two could reconcile, but after two years of the still sizzling affair he relented. Ten days after the Fishers' Mexican divorce was granted, Elizabeth and Richard were married in Montreal on March 15, 1964, by a Unitarian minister in a suite at the Ritz-Carlton hotel. Elizabeth wore yellow chiffon and her long black hair was adorned with white hyacinths.

For 10 years, the Burtons made movies, many of them together; unceasingly provided the gossip columnists prodigious material about which to write; and bounced from one exotic locale to the next. Booze flowed and both suffered the consequences. Their relationship in tatters, the Burtons divorced in 1974. A year later they remarried while on a safari in Botswana, taking the world by surprise. In 1976, they divorced for a second time. The couple did not have children, but Richard did adopt Elizabeth's two daughters: Liza, her daughter with Mike Todd, and Maria, the daughter that she and Eddie Fisher had adopted from Germany. The Fishers' marriage dissolved before the adoption could be finalized.

With Roger Moore in The Last Time I Saw Paris, *released in 1954; opposite page, a studio photo from the same film*

In 1976, the same year that Elizabeth and Richard Burton called it quits, Elizabeth married ex-Secretary of the Navy John Warner, soon to be elected a U.S. Senator from Virginia. Throwing aside her movie star persona, Elizabeth jumped at the chance to get muddy at Warner's rural Virginia farm. But tractor riding and politicking did not entertain her for long and the couple divorced in 1982. Soon thereafter, Elizabeth checked herself into the Betty Ford Center for seven weeks from December 1983 to January 1984 to address her dependency on alcohol and prescription painkillers. In the late 1980s, she returned for further treatment.

Almost a decade passed before Elizabeth married again, this time for the last time. During her second stay at the Betty Ford Center, she met Larry Fortensky, a construction worker 20 years her junior. The two were married on October 6, 1991, at Neverland Ranch in California, the home of Michael Jackson, Elizabeth's very close friend and confidante. It was a star-studded, paparazzi-covered, hugely costly event. They were divorced after five years, but remained friendly until Elizabeth's death. It was rumored that the couple's prenuptial agreement gave Larry a $1 million settlement after five years of marriage.

1955

During the making of Giant, *1955, this page and opposite*

AWARDS AND HONORS

Elizabeth Taylor won her first major award for acting in 1957 at the 14th Golden Globe Awards. She was given the Special Achievement Award for consistent performance. As if to bear out that claim, she then began a string of notable performances for which she received numerous nominations in the U.S. and abroad. She was nominated for the Academy Award, Best Actress, for her performance in *Raintree County* (1957), *Cat on a Hot Tin Roof* (1958), *Suddenly, Last Summer* (1959), and *BUtterfield 8* (1960). She won for the last film, *BUtterfield 8*.

She also won the Laurel Award (created by *Motion Picture Exhibitor* magazine) for Top Female Dramatic Performance for the same four films. She was awarded the David di Donatello Golden Plate Award from the Academy of Italian Cinema for her portrayal of Catherine Holly in *Suddenly, Last Summer*. For her performance as Maggie "the Cat" in *Cat on a Hot Tin Roof*, Elizabeth was nominated by BAFTA (British Academy Film Award) for Best Actress in a Leading Role. Rounding out the list were two nominations for the Bambi Award (oldest media award in Germany) for Best International Actress for the two films: *Suddenly, Last Summer* and *BUtterfield 8*.

For her performance in *The Sandpiper*, in which she starred opposite her then husband Richard Burton in 1965, Elizabeth won the Laurel Award for Top Female Dramatic Performance. But Elizabeth's *piece de resistance* was her outstanding dramatic performance as Martha in *Who's Afraid of Virginia Woolf?* which was released in 1966. For the film, she won an amazing seven awards for best actress, including the Oscar, BAFTA, Bambi, Kansas City Film Critics Circle Award, Laurel, National Board of Review Award, and the New York Film Critics Circle Award (she tied with Lynn Redgrave for *Georgy Girl* for this last award). In addition, she was nominated for a Golden Globe for Best Actress in a Motion Picture Drama, but lost to Anouk Aimée for *A Man and a Woman*.

Elizabeth and Rock Hudson, one of her Giant co-stars, leave their imprints in wet cement at Grauman's Chinese Theater on September 26, 1956

Above, with husband Mike Todd at a party to celebrate the Around the World in 80 Days *Best Picture Oscar; he produced the film. Right, a publicity still for the Southern epic* Raintree County, *which failed miserably at the box office, but garnered Elizabeth her first Academy Award nomination for Best Actress, 1958; she lost to Joanne Woodward for* The Three Faces of Eve.

A little kiss from third husband Mike Todd

After this spate of awards, the momentum of Elizabeth Taylor's career began to slow. In 1967, for *The Taming of the Shrew*, she again took home the David di Donatello Award for Best Foreign Actress, tying with Julie Christie for her performance in *Doctor Zhivago*, and was also nominated for a BAFTA for Best Actress in a Leading Role, also for *The Taming of the Shrew*. In 1972, she once more won the David di Donatello Award for Best Foreign Actress for her role as Zee Blakely in *X,Y, and Zee*. The same year, she was honored with the Silver Bear (Berlin National Film Festival) for Best Actress for the movie *Hammersmith Is Out*. A year later, *Ash Wednesday* garnered her a nomination for Golden Globe Best Actress in a Motion Picture Drama.

Elizabeth's appearance in *The Little Foxes* in 1981, her first serious work on the stage, was rewarded with a Tony Award nomination for Best Actress in a play. The tour began in Fort Lauderdale, Florida, before moving quickly to Washington D.C., New York City, New Orleans, Los Angeles, and finally to London. It played

Elizabeth, Mike Todd, and their newborn daughter, Liza, photographed by Toni Frissell, 1957

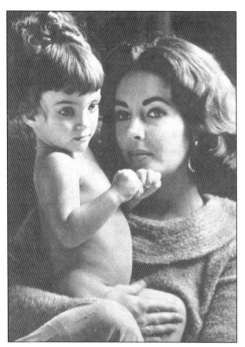
Elizabeth holding her daughter Liza Todd

to a sold-out house at the Martin Beck Theater on Broadway.

In 2000, Queen Elizabeth II of England bestowed on "Queen Elizabeth of the Cinema" the title of Dame of the British Empire. In addition, Elizabeth was honored with a Film Society of Lincoln Center Gala Tribute in 1986 and received the Kennedy Center Honor in 2002.

For achievement in her profession, she also was honored with Harvard University's Hasty Pudding Theatricals Woman of the Year in 1977, Cecil B. DeMille Award given by the Hollywood Foreign Press (Golden Globe Awards) in 1985, Women in Film Crystal Award in 1985, American Film Institute Life Achievement Award in 1993, Screen Actors Guild Life Achievement Award in 1998, BAFTA Fellowship Award in 1999, and BAFTA/LA Cunard Britannia Award for Artistic Excellence in International Entertainment in 2005.

During filming of Suddenly, Last Summer, *1959*

For her energetic and faithful efforts on behalf of AmfAR (The Foundation for AIDS Research), Elizabeth was given the Simon Wiesenthal Distinguished Service Award in 1980, Legion d'Honneur (France) in 1988, Prince of Asturias Award (Spain) in 1992, Jean Hersholt Humanitarian Award by the Academy of Motion Picture Arts and Sciences, and GLAAD (Gay and Lesbian Alliance Against Defamation) Vanguard Award.

47

Marrying Eddie Fisher, her fourth husband, in 1959, at a synagogue in Las Vegas; Elizabeth had earlier converted to Judaism as a form of consolation after Mike Todd's untimely death.

HER JEWELRY

When Elizabeth Taylor agreed to be associated with a perfume, it was named White Diamonds in tribute to her marvelously vast—at her death it was estimated to be worth $150 million—and quite famous jewelry collection about which she wrote in her book *My Love Affair with Jewelry*, published in 2002. Her third and fifth husbands, Mike Todd and Richard Burton, respectively, were primarily responsible for the growth and magnificence of her jewelry box.

In December 2011, Christie's exhibited over 250 pieces of Elizabeth's jewelry prior to an auction whose proceeds benefited the Elizabeth Taylor Aids Foundation. The sale of all 1,778 lots shattered many records. A few of the records broken were the highest price for a pearl jewel ("La Peregrina," the 203-grain, 16th-century pearl on a pearl, ruby, and diamond necklace designed by Cartier specifically for Elizabeth and believed to be over 500 years old, previously owned and worn by Spanish royals (in photo at right)), the highest per carat price for a colorless diamond (the Elizabeth Taylor Diamond, the 33.19-carat, potentially flawless diamond set on a ring Elizabeth wore nearly everyday), the highest price for an Indian jewel (the heart-shaped Taj Mahal Diamond, a gift from Richard Burton to Elizabeth on her fortieth birthday, believed to have been given by Shah Jahan to his favorite wife for whom he built the Taj Mahal in Agra, India), and the highest price per carat for a ruby. The diamond tiara that Mike Todd gave her sold for $4.2 million. Total auction proceeds were $156,756,576, far exceeding pre-sale expectations. Every item auctioned was sold. Twenty-six pieces sold for more than $1 million each.

A wink for her fans in Rome, 1961, after a pneumonia scare that required a tracheotomy to allow her to breathe; the bandage over the incision can be seen in this photo. The small scar that remained was later removed by cosmetic surgery.

Husband Eddie Fisher holding Elizabeth and Elizabet holding her Best Actress Oscar for BUtterfield 8 *in 1962*

After winning the Academy Award for Best Actress for her role in BUtterfield 8, *1962*

With her fourth husband,
Eddie Fisher, in 1962

Two stills from Cleopatra, *above and right, 1963*

A scene from The V.I.P.s *with Richard Burton, released in 1963*

With Richard Burton

*Liz and Dick on the grounds of
La Fiorintina, Saint-Jean-Cap-Ferrat, in
France; photo by Henry Clarke, 1967*

*Liz and
Dick tie
the kno[
for the
first tim[
in 1964[*

In The Taming of the Shrew, *1967*

After winning the Academy Award for Best Actress for her role in Who's Afraid of Virginia Woolf?, *1967*

WHAT LIZ (OOPS!) SAID

"Big girls need big diamonds."

"I don't ever remember not being famous."

"I am a very committed wife. And I should be committed too - for being married so many times."

"Everything makes me nervous - except making films."

"I've only slept with men I've been married to. How many women can make that claim?"

"If someone's dumb enough to offer me a million dollars to make a picture, I'm certainly not dumb enough to turn it down."

"Some of my best leading men have been dogs and horses."

"Success is a great deodorant."

"You find out who your real friends are when you're involved in a scandal."

"It's not the having, it's the getting."

"People who know me well, call me Elizabeth. I dislike Liz."

At the side of her sixth husband, Virginia Senator John Warner, being introduced to Queen Elizabeth II and President Gerald R. Ford at the White House

Volunteering with the Red Cross as a member of the Ladies of the United States Senate

Elizabeth listens to an animated Bette Davis at the Filmex-sponsored
"An Evening with Elizabeth Taylor" in November 1981

OF A CERTAIN AGE

W hen Elizabeth died from congestive heart failure on March 23, 2011, in Los Angeles' Cedars-Sinai Medical Center at the age of 79, the world mourned. All four of her children—Michael Wilding, Christopher Wilding, Eliza Todd Tivey, and Maria Burton—were by her side. She is buried in the Great Mausoleum, where public access is restricted, at Forest Lawn Memorial Park in Glendale, California.

All of her life Elizabeth was plagued with physical ailments and injuries, some quite serious. According to her *Los Angeles Times* and Associated Press obituaries, respectively, she was hospitalized 70 times and underwent 20 major surgeries. These two news agencies also reported that she broke her back five times, punctured her esophagus, and had both hips replaced. Her surgeries included a hysterectomy and removal of a benign brain tumor.

Elizabeth smoked cigarettes into her mid-fifties, which may have contributed to her frequent bouts of pneumonia throughout her life, one of which required an emergency tracheotomy. She also suffered from skin cancer. In 1983,

In Boston, May 1983, where she and Richard Burton starred in Noel Coward's play Private Lives *as a benefit for the Metropolitan Center*

Bob Hope performs with Elizabeth in a USO show aboard the aircraft carrier USS Lexington during the celebration of the 75th anniversary of naval aviation in 1986.

71

when she was admitted to the Betty Ford Center for the first time, she confessed that she had struggled with alcoholism and prescription drug abuse for most of her life. Elizabeth's problems with addictive behavior were also evident in her enormous fluctuations in weight over short periods of time. All of these conditions contributed to her ill health. At the end of her life, she depended on a wheelchair to move around, because congestive heart failure—diagnosed in 2004—slowed the blood flow to her lower extremities, especially her ankles and feet, making walking difficult.

At the American Film Festival in Deauville, France, in September 1985

In 1993, receiving the Lifetime Achievement Award from the American Film Institute

Testifying before the Labor, Health, and Human services Senate Subcommittee on May 8, 1986

On September 28, 2006, when she delivered the state of AIDS address at the 2006 Macy's Passport gala in Santa Monica, California

75

NATIONAL VELVET
(1944)

A story of triumphing over long odds, *National Velvet* is the tale of a 12-year-old British girl named Velvet who wins a horse in a raffle. With the help of a young drifter played by Mickey Rooney, she trains her new horse to compete in the Grand National. At the last minute, Velvet replaces the jockey, believing that she has a better chance of winning the race. And she is right. She wins the race before she is discovered to be a young women disguised as a male jockey.

Cast & Credits:
Mickey Rooney—Mi Taylor
Donald Crisp—Mr. Herbert Brown
Elizabeth Taylor—Velvet Brown
Anne Revere—Mrs. Araminty Brown
Angela Lansbury—Edwina Brown

Directed by Clarence Brown
Produced by Pandro S. Berman
Screenplay by Helen Deutsch, based on
       National Velvet by Enid Bagnold
Music by Herbert Stothart
Cinematography by Leonard Smith
Studio—MGM
Released on December 14, 1944

With Mickey Rooney sitting behind her

FATHER OF THE BRIDE (1950)

This film recounts every father's nightmare when he discovers not only that his daughter has given her heart to another man and is getting married, but that he will have to foot the bill for a lavish, no-holes-barred celebration. *Father of the Bride* coincided with Elizabeth's first and short-lived marriage at the age of 18 to Nicky Hilton of the Hilton hotel chain. The marriage was conveniently encouraged by MGM.

Cast & Credits:
Spencer Tracy—Stanley T. Banks
Elizabeth Taylor—Kay Banks
Joan Bennett—Ellie Banks

Directed by Vincente Minnelli
Produced by Pandro S. Berman
Screenplay by Frances Goodrich and
    Albert Hackett, based on *Father of the
    Bride* by Edward Streeter
Music by Adolph Deutsch
Cinematography by John Alton
Studio—MGM
Released on June 16, 1950

78

With Spencer Tracy, who played the father of the bride

A PLACE IN THE SUN (1951)

ritically acclaimed, *A Place in the Sun* won six Academy Awards as well as the first ever Golden Globe for Best Motion Picture-Drama. A remake of the 1931 *An American Tragedy* based on the novel of the same name by Theodore Dreiser, the plot centers on the two women who tempt the character portrayed by Montgomery Clift: one a "society" girl (Elizabeth Taylor) and the other a factory worker (Shelley Winters). Ultimately, the love triangle ends with the death of Alice, the factory worker.

Cast & Credits:
Montgomery Clift—George Eastman
Elizabeth Taylor—Angela Vickers
Shelley Winters—Alice Trip

Directed by George Stevens
Produced by George Stevens
Screenplay by Michael Wilson and
    Harry Brown, based on *An American
    Tragedy* by Theodore Dreiser
Music by Franz Waxman
Cinematography by William C. Mellor
Studio—Paramount Pictures
Released on August 14, 1951

Elizabeth Taylor
Montgomery Clift
in Academy Award
Winner
George Stevens'
production of
the deeply
moving story
of ill-fated
young love!

PARAMOUNT
PRESENTS

Elizabeth Taylor
Montgomery Clift
Shelley Winters
George Stevens'
PRODUCTION OF
A PLACE IN THE SUN

WITH KEEFE BRASSELLE
PRODUCED AND DIRECTED BY GEORGE STEVENS
SCREENPLAY BY MICHAEL WILSON AND HARRY BROWN
BASED ON THE NOVEL AN AMERICAN TRAGEDY BY THEODORE DREISER
AND THE PLAY BY PATRICK KEARNEY ADAPTED FROM THE NOVEL
A PARAMOUNT RE-RELEASE

The photographs of Elizabeth Taylor and Montgomery Clift taken as publicity shots for A Place in the Sun *have been touted as some of the most beautiful ever caught on film.*

GIANT
(1956)

G iant is a family saga set on the broad plains of Texas during the years leading up to and following World War II. In 2005, the National Film Registry selected the film for preservation because of its cultural, historical and aesthetic significance.

Cast & Credits:
Elizabeth Taylor—Leslie Benedict
Rock Hudson—Bick Benedict
James Dean—Jett Rink

Directed by George Stevens
Produced by George Stevens
Screenplay by Fred Guiol and Ivan Moffat, based on *Giant* by Edna Ferber
Music by Dimitri Tiomkin
Cinematography by William C. Mellor
Studio—Warner Brothers
Released on October 10, 1956

With co-star James Dean

With co-star Rock Hudson

THE ORIGINAL FULL-LENGTH VERSION

GIANT

ELIZABETH TAYLOR · ROCK HUDSON
JAMES DEAN

Released by Kino International Corporation

CAT ON A HOT TIN ROOF (1958)

O ne of the top ten box office hits of 1958, *Cat on a Hot Tin Roof* was the perfect vehicle for sultry, tempestuous Elizabeth Taylor in her role as the daughter-in-law of a wealthy Southern patriarch dying of cancer. The secret in the family is her boozing husband's (Paul Newman) unrequited love for his boyhood friend, Skipper, who has committed suicide.

Cast & Credits:
Elizabeth Taylor—Maggie Pollitt
Paul Newman—Brick Pollitt
Burl Ives—Big Daddy Pollitt
Judith Anderson—Big Momma Pollitt
Jack Carson—Gooper Pollitt
Madeleine Sherwood—Mae Flynn Pollitt

Directed by Richard Brooks
Produced by Laurence Weingarten
Screenplay by Richard Brooks and
  James Poe, based on the Pulitzer-
  winning play by Tennessee Williams
Cinematography by William Daniels
Studio—MGM
Released on September 20, 1958

With Paul Newman

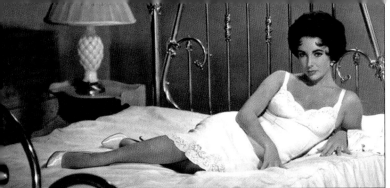

Left, the cast, top to bottom:
Jack Carson, Madeleine
Sherwood, Burl Ives, Judith
Anderson, Paul Newman,
Elizabeth Taylor

SUDDENLY, LAST SUMMER (1959)

K atherine Hepburn and Elizabeth Taylor both received nominations for Best Actress by the Academy of Motion Picture Arts and Sciences (Oscar) and the Golden Globes for their work in *Suddenly, Last Summer*. The Oscar went to Simone Signoret for *Room at the Top*, but Elizabeth took home the Golden Globe. The story revolves around the mysterious death of Catherine's (Elizabeth) cousin, which she witnessed, and the mystery's eventual unravelling.

Cast & Credits:
Elizabeth Taylor—Catherine Holly
Katherine Hepburn—Violet Venable
Montgomery Clift—Dr. John Cukrowicz

Directed by Joseph L. Mankiewicz
Produced by Sam Spiegel
Screenplay by Gore Vidal, based on the play of the same name by Tennessee Williams
Music by Buxton Orr and Malcolm Arnold
Cinematography by Jack Hildyard
Studio—Columbia Pictures
Released on December 22, 1959

Katherine Hepburn, Montgomery Clift, and Elizabeth Taylor

THESE
ARE
POWERS
AND
PASSIONS
WITHOUT
PRECEDENT
IN MOTION
PICTURES
!

ELIZABETH   KATHARINE   MONTGOMERY
TAYLOR · HEPBURN · CLIFT

TENNESSEE
WILLIAMS

JOSEPH L.
MANKIEWICZ

SAM
SPIEGEL

BUTTERFIELD 8
(1960)

A woman (Elizabeth's Gloria Wandrous) whose name is in many men's little black books seeks a new start, but chased by her demons she never makes it. Elizabeth won one of her two Best Actress Oscars for this role. The novel on which the screenplay is based was inspired by the mysterious death of a New York woman in 1931.

Cast & Credits:
Elizabeth Taylor—Gloria Wandrous
Laurence Harvey—Weston Liggett
Eddie Fisher—Steve Carpenter
Dina Merrill—Emily Liggett

Directed by Daniel Mann
Produced by Pandro S. Berman
Screenplay by John Michael Hayes and
    Charles Schnee, based on the novel of
    the same name by John O'Hara
Music by Bronislau Kaper
Cinematography by Charles Harten and
    Joseph Ruttenberg
Studio—MGM
Released on November 4, 1960

CLEOPATRA
(1963)

Taking a break in filming with Richard Burton

Cleopatra—the story of the infamous Egyptian queen—was the highest grossing film of 1963, but failed to make a profit because it was also one of the most expensive films ever made. It received mixed reviews from the critics. Elizabeth Taylor received $1 million and 10 percent of the gross, at that time a groundbreaking amount of compensation.

Cast & Credits:
Elizabeth Taylor—Cleopatra
Richard Burton—Mark Antony
Rex Harrison—Julius Ceasar
Roddy McDowall—Augustus

Directed by Joseph L. Mankiewicz
Produced by Walter Wanger
Screenplay by Joseph L. Mankiewicz,
    Ranald MacDougall, Sidney Buchman
Music by Alex North
Cinematography by Leon Shamroy
Studio—20th Century Fox
Released on June 12, 1963

THE SANDPIPER
(1965)

The new Mr. and Mrs. Richard Burton starred in an ill-fated love story between an unconventional, unwed mother of a young son and an Episcopal priest. The film is set in Big Sur, California, and won an Oscar for Best Original Song, "The Shadow of Your Smile."

Cast & Credits:
Elizabeth Taylor—Laura Reynolds
Richard Burton—Dr. Edward Hewitt
Eva Marie Saint—Claire Hewitt
Charles Bronson—Cos Erickson

Directed by Vincente Minnelli
Produced by Martin Ransohoff
Screenplay by Irene and Louis Kamp,
    Michael Wilson, and Dalton Trumbo
Music by Johnny Mandel
Cinematography by Milton R. Krasner
Studio—MGM
Released on June 3, 1965

With co-star Richard Burton, opposite page; movie poster, left

WHO'S AFRAID OF VIRGINIA WOOLF?
(1966)

A young couple, Nick and Honey, are unwittingly dragged into the vitriolic battles, fueled by alcohol, of their hosts, a middle-aged married couple, Martha and George, whose codependence locks them unashamedly into endless rounds of abusive arguments. Elizabeth Taylor won her second Best Actress Oscar for her performance in this film.

Cast & Credits:
Elizabeth Taylor—Martha
Richard Burton—George
George Segal—Nick
Sandy Dennis—Honey

Directed by Mike Nichols
Produced by Ernest Lehman
Screenplay by Ernest Lehman based on
    the play by Edward Albee
Music by Alex North
Cinematography by Haskell Wexler
Studio—Warner Brothers
Released on June 22, 1966

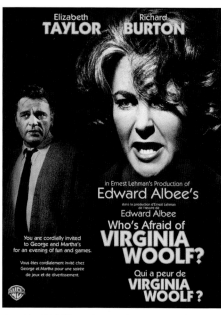

An English/French movie poster, above; a scene with Richard Burton, top right, and a break in filming showing a relaxed Taylor and Burton, bottom right

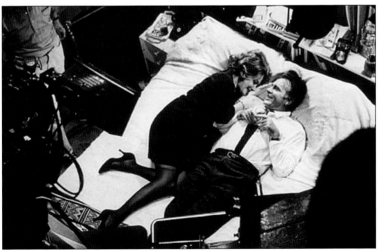

HER MAJOR FILMS

FILM (Release Date)	CO-STARS	DIRECTOR
Lassie Come Home (1943)	Roddy McDowall, Donald Crisp, Edmund Gwenn	Fred M. Wilcox
Jane Eyre (1944)	Orson Wells, Joan Fontaine	Robert Stevenson
The White Cliffs of Dover (1944)	Irene Dunne, Alan Marshal	Clarence Brown
National Velvet (1944)	Mickey Rooney, Donald Crisp, Angela Lansbury	Clarence Brown
Life with Father (1947)	William Powell, Irene Dunne	Michael Curtiz
A Date with Judy (1948)	Wallace Beery, Jane Powell, Carmen Miranda	Richard Thorpe
Little Women (1949)	June Allyson, Janet Leigh, Margaret O'Brien	Mervyn LeRoy
Father of the Bride (1950)	Spencer Tracy, Joan Bennett	Vincente Minnelli
Father's Little Dividend (1951)	Spencer Tracy, Joan Bennett	Vincente Minnelli
A Place in the Sun (1951)	Montgomery Clift, Shelley Winters	George Stevens
Ivanhoe (1952)	Robert Taylor, Joan Fontaine	Richard Thorpe
The Girl Who Had Everything (1953)	Fernando Lamas, William Powell	Richard Thorpe
Beau Brummell (1954)	Stewart Granger, Peter Ustinov	Curtis Bernhardt
The Last Time I Saw Paris (1954)	Van Johnson, Walter Pidgeon, Donna Reed	Richard Brooks
Giant (1956)	Rock Hudson, James Dean, Carroll Baker	George Stevens
Raintree County (1957)	Montgomery Clift, Eva Marie Saint, Lee Marvin	Edward Dmytryk
Cat on a Hot Tin Roof (1958)	Paul Newman, Burl Ives, Judith Anderson	Richard Brooks
Suddenly, Last Summer (1959)	Katherine Hepburn, Montgomery Clift	Joseph L. Mankiewicz
BUtterfield 8 (1960)	Laurence Harvey, Eddie Fisher, Dina Merrill	Daniel Mann
Cleopatra (1963)	Richard Burton, Rex Harrison, Roddy McDowall	Joseph L. Mankiewicz
The V.I.P.s (1963)	Richard Burton, Louis Jourdan, Maggie Smith	Anthony Asquith
The Sandpiper (1965)	Richard Burton, Eva Marie Saint, Charles Bronson	Vincente Minnelli
Who's Afraid of Virginia Woolf? (1966)	Richard Burton, George Segal, Sandy Dennis	Mike Nichols
The Taming of the Shrew (1967)	Richard Burton, Natasha Pyne, Michael Hordern	Franco Zeffirelli
Doctor Faustus (1967)	Richard Burton, Andreas Teuber	Richard Burton/Nevill Coghill
Reflections in a Golden Eye (1967)	Marlon Brando, Brian Keith, Julie Harris	John Huston
The Comedians (1967)	Richard Burton, Alec Guinness, Peter Ustinov	Peter Glenville
Boom! (1968)	Richard Burton, Noel Coward, Joanna Shimkus	Joseph Losey
Secret Ceremony (1968)	Mia Farrow, Robert Mitchum	Joseph Losey
X, Y, and Zee (1972)	Michael Caine, Susannah York	Brian G. Hutton
Hammersmith Is Out (1972)	Richard Burton, Peter Ustinov, Beau Bridges	Peter Ustinov
Divorce His, Divorce Hers (1973)	Richard Burton, Carrie Nye, Barry Foster	Waris Hussein
Ash Wednesday (1973)	Henry Fonda, Helmut Berger	Larry Peerce
The Blue Bird (1976)	Jane Fonda, Ava Gardner, Cicely Tyson	George Cukor
Victory at Entebbe (1976)	Anthony Hopkins, Burt Lancaster, Julie Harris	Marvin J. Chomsky
The Mirror Crack'd (1980)	Angela Lansbury, Kim Novak, Rock Hudson	Guy Hamilton